UKIYO-E

CONTENTS

Published by
CASTLE BOOKS
A Division of
BOOK SALES, INC.
110 Enterprise Avenue
Secaucus, New Jersey 07094

GLOSSARY OF JAPANESE TERMS

beni-e	red pictures; a term used to describe hand-colored prints
benzuri-e	red-printed pictures, a woodcut of two or three printed colors made from corresponding wood-blocks; these were a stepping stone in the development of polychrome prints
Edo	original name of the city of Tokyo, where ukiyo-e prints were born
hashira-e	long narrow pictures designed to be hung on pillars or screen panels
Kabuki	the popular theater of Japan, combining the disciplines of drama, music, mime and dance
kakemono-e	hanging scroll pictures, weighted at the bottom, used as interior decoration
kamuro	an apprentice to an oiran in a Yoshiwara house
manga	sketchbook, and name of Hokusai's famous fifteen-volume treatise
nishiki-e	brocade pictures, the name of the polychrome or many-colored woodblock print made from numerous woodblocks
Noh	the classical theater of Japan, a more ascetic form than Kabuki, but to which the Kabuki theater owes its origins
oiran	courtesan in a Yoshiwara house
ronin	a mercenary samurai, not in service to a warlord
samisen	a Japanese musical instrument resembling a lute
samurai	the warrior class, usually in service to a warlord
shogun	the ruling feudal warlord
shunga	pictures of an erotic nature
sumi	an ink used for writing and drawing, obtained from an ink stick moistened with water
Torii	the clan of painters found by Kiyonobu
uki-e	perspective pictures, based on Western theories of art
ukiyo-e	pictures of the floating world, the name for the woodcuts of popular subject matter, originally considered decadent by the ruling classes
urushi-e	glazed pictures, made by mixing glue with black ink
Utagawa	the clan of painters founded by Toyoharu
Yoshiwara	the pleasure district of Edo, center of the brothels, or green houses, which flourished from 1615-1957

INTRODUCTION

Ukiyo-e, which translates as "pictures of the floating world," is a particularly Japanese phenomenon. Born as an underground movement, restricted by the ruling classes to the lowest elements of society, it grew in both technique and popularity until, ironically, it developed into the artistic form most representative of Japanese art to the outside world.

Seventeenth-century Japan was ruled by a government of feudal warlords, the Tokugawa Shogunate, with the figurehead emperor safely tucked away in his palace in Kyoto. In the city of Edo (later to be known as Tokyo), however, there was a rising merchant class, growing in wealth. The shogunate, which dictated all matters of social class in Japan, deemed it unworthy to be a merchant or tradesman, and recognized only the priest and samurai or warrior classes as the true aristocracy of Japan. The pursuits and pleasures of the merchant classes were strictly limited; they had no real social position and their wealth could not buy prestige or power. In effect, they were limited to the pursuit of materialistic gratification as the only outlet for their newly acquired wealth. The term *ukiyo,* from a Buddhist word meaning "the floating world," became a derisory name for the pleasures of money and material things—the transitory items of this life, unworthy in terms of the striving of the soul for perfect harmony with the universe.

The urban merchants did thrive, however, and within the strictures placed upon them by the feudal overlords, there arose a bustling and healthy urban culture, based on the two strong stanchions of Kabuki theater and the Yoshiwara brothel district. In time, ukiyo came to be synonymous with the Edo pleasure quarters and the ukiyo-e, or "pictures of the floating world," which depicted the thriving theater and courtesan houses, became a sought-after commodity.

Ukiyo-e were prepared as woodblock prints, and were intended both as posters advertising certain events and as a popular art form for the masses, who were likely to pin them up as decoration on the folding screens in their homes. They were not considered high art and the craftsmen who worked on them were not accorded the status of fine artists. Most artisans, in fact, worked under the aegis of a publisher, a businessman who knew the popular taste.

It is important to look at the Kabuki theater to understand the tradition of ukiyo-e. Theatrical presentations combined the arts of drama, dance, song and music, delivered with broad gestures that used mime, exaggerated facial expression and spoken oratory, aided by elaborate costumes; often they would last an entire day. The plays were well-known to their patrons and repeated over and over, with families of actors often playing a certain character for generations, much in the same manner as the *commedia dell' arte* tradition in Europe. Male actors would also play the female roles. Ukiyo-e prints and Kabuki theater had a symbiotic relationship—Kabuki producers sought the publication of prints that would advertise their productions and build the reputations of their actors; ukiyo-e publishers looked to the Kabuki for new subject matter that would appeal to their customers.

The Yoshiwara, or brothel district, provided the other great source of inspiration for ukiyo-e. The Yoshiwara brothels, or "green houses," played a large role in the life of the Edo merchants, almost all of whom patronized them. Edo has had the reputation of being one of the most openly licentious cities in history, largely because of the government-sanctioned Yoshiwara district, and the ukiyo-e took much of its subject matter from the women and activities of the Yoshiwara houses. If the portraits of Kabuki actors glorified men, the Yoshiwara pictures celebrated women—following their daily lives, their training, their skills, their beauty, in pictures that were both delicate and charming, and could also be surprisingly intimate and erotic. But whereas the Kabuki portraits were depictions of specific actors, the Yoshiwara pictures rarely centered on the features or gestures of individual women. They were more likely to be glorifications of intricately patterned kimonos, or later, an idealized representation of feminine perfection.

As ukiyo-e became more and more an accepted feature of Japanese life, it grew more sophisticated in technique and subject matter, with the original hand-colored woodcuts gradually giving way to more complex printing techniques and subject matter expanding to include themes of Japanese history, landscapes, studies of birds and animals, and ghost and horror stories. By the nineteenth century, when the carefully isolated and protected island of Japan at last encouraged commerce with the outside world, it was these ukiyo-e prints which were to give the Western world a glimpse of Japanese life, and which would become, with their simplicity of line and large flat areas of color, a major influence on the more innovative European painters.

Although ukiyo-e refers to subject matter, and can be taken to represent painted as well as printed pictures, the most common reference is to woodblock prints. This technique was originally imported, like so many other things Japanese, from China. In the early stages the ukiyo-e prints were printed in black, with any other colors hand-painted. In the eighteenth century great strides in technique were made: by mid-century woodblock prints of three colors were achieved by the artist Harunobu and a generation later, the first five-or-more color prints were created. The polychrome print was known as a *nishiki-e,* or brocade painting. Nishiki-e originated as brush drawings on thin paper, which were then placed face-down on wooden blocks. The paper was rubbed with transparent tissue covered with oil to make the image transparent. The image was then carved into the wooden block and ink applied to the raised portions. Two marks were cut into the block as printing registers. When a proof was pulled off the key block, instructions for printing and areas of color were indicated in red ink for the printer. The various artisans involved in this process worked as a team in the shop of a publisher, who would affix his signature seal, along with that of the government censor, to the finished work. The output of an accomplished printer could be as much as 200 sheets a day of popular subjects.

6

Although no one member of the production team was accorded more status than any other, it is nevertheless the designers whose names we now remember and who have been credited with the art of ukiyo-e.

The first known ukiyo-e artist was Moronobu, and the early or primitive phase of ukiyo-e woodcuts is dominated by his remarkable achievements in book illustration and single-sheet woodcuts, the first of their kind. Kiyonobu, the founder of the Torii clan of painters which would dominate the field of theatrical portraits and posters for generations, added his achievements to those of Moronobu in the development of the early hand-colored ukiyo-e prints. The artists Masonobu and Toyonobu took the process a step further, refining line and developing more advanced printing techniques called *benizuri-e,* or two and three color printings.

The golden age of ukiyo-e witnessed the development of the nishiki-e, or brocade pictures, by Harunobu. As carving and printing techniques became more sophisticated, so did the draftsmanship of the designer, now allowed refinement and delicacy of line. A new concern with realism emerged in the work of Harunobu and in that of his successors, Shunsho, Kiyonaga, Utamaro and Sharaku, whose work was incresingly based on real models in real settings.

The last three decades of the eighteenth century, which saw the success of these great masters of ukiyo-e, was a prosperous era, although one in which social conditions became increasingly unsettled. By the turn of the century, political crises were rampant and a movement arose for the restoration of the emperor and an overthrow of the shogun—an event that did occur in the mid-nineteenth century. As the stronghold of the shogunate became more and more shaky, government censors became increasingly harsh, imposing bans on artists and subject matter. Chafing under these conditions, artists became more aware of the influences that were slowly creeping into Japan from the West. Artists of the Utagawa school, founded by Toyoharu, developed *uki-e,* perspective prints based on Dutch copperplate engravings. The Utagawa school managed to retain dominance for another generation through the work of Toyohiro and Toyokuni, but their art remained strongly traditional, stifled by government censorship.

During the first half of the nineteenth century, two artists, Hokusai and Hiroshige, emerged to become the undisputed masters of the ukiyo-e woodcut, and their beautiful pictures brought the Japanese woodcut to world attention.

Hokusai was, above all else, a great individualist, whose artistic vision encompassed a complete range of subject matter and who created works that combined the best qualities of centuries of Japanese artists with his own remarkable insights. A generation later, Hiroshige, the consummate landscape painter who based his work on realistic studies made on travels throughout Japan, would add his work to that of Hokusai. By the end of the nineteenth century, the art of ukiyo-e would delight Western artists and collectors to a degree that made the names of the masters of the woodblock print well-known far beyond the shores of Japan.

MORONOBU

The earliest of the ukiyo-e woodcut artists known to us was Hishikawa Moronobu (1618 or 1625-1694), a book illustrator who began to produce individual prints, freed from the bound volume. Ukiyo-e prints were dominated by Moronobu and his followers, known as the Hishikawa school, until the end of the seventeenth century. Moronobu first began to sign his prints as individual subjects around 1672. His themes were at first mainly confined to life in the Yoshiwara brothels, but as he became more secure in his reputation, he expanded his subject matter to include epic historical and mythological themes and travel subjects. Moronobu was the son of an embroidery artist, and as a child he learned embroidery techniques and then began to draw and paint. His first major achievement was in introducing the wood-cut book illustration to the city of Edo from Kyoto and Osaka, where the technique had been developed a century before. As a result, the woodcut-illustrated book, previously a treasured possession of the nobleman, now became available to the merchant classes in the city of Edo and Moronobu was credited with being the inventor of the form. He was certainly the first artist to portray the life he saw around him in the Yoshiwara brothels and the theater. He was also the first naturalist woodcut artist of plants and wildlife, often annotating books on these subjects with texts of his own. Another important aspect of his work was the *Shunga*. Shungas were books of an erotic nature depicting sexual aspects of life in the Yoshiwara district in a natural and uninhibited manner. Moronobu became a priest late in his life, entering a monastery at Edo, but even during this time continued the publication of the shunga, an example of the open attitude of the Japanese people toward the erotic. The emergence of the woodcut as an independant art form, separate from the format of a book, was encouraged by the theatrical directors of the Kabuki and the proprietors of the Yoshiwara houses, who benefitted from the publicity. Moronobu was the first of many artists who were to popularize this unique new art form. When he died, soon after retiring to the monastery, he left over 108 books as well as innumberable single sheet pictures and brush paintings. In his pictures of the everyday life of the city of Edo, Moronobu virtually established the ukiyo-e style—the "pictures of the floating world."

Woman Standing Beside a Cherry Tree (ca. 1688-90)
This panel is a fine example of an early ukiyo-e woodcut. Drawn in *sumi*, an inking style adopted from the Chinese, it was printed in black and hand colored in yellow, light brown and a peach-colored red tint, and highlighted with white lead. The portrait, executed with a delicate line and flat pattern, portrays a woman in an elaborate holiday-dress kimono, with her hair dressed in the style of women of the court. The season of the year is indicated in the blossoms on the gnarled old tree behind her.

KIYONOBU

The dominance of Moronobu and his followers of the Hishikawa school was broken by the emergence of the great Torii clan of painters, whose founder and greatest artist was Torii Kiyonobu (1664-1729). The Torii artists rose to prominence as celebrators of the Kabuki, producing posters of the greatest actors of the Kabuki theater, and virtually monopolizing theatrical poster prints for one hundred and fifty years. Kiyonobu furthered the art developed by Moronobu with a process of hand-coloring prints with an orange pigment, a technique that was in use by the end of Moronobu's career and can be seen in the prints on this and the preceding page. By the mid-eighteenth century, Kiyonobu's followers and students, the second generation of Torii, pioneered several new techniques, including *beni-e,* hand-colored red pictures, which used pigments of red, green and purple as well as yellow, and *urushi-e,* in which glue was mixed with the black ink to give it a shiny, lacquered effect. Kiyonobu developed a style marked by a unique method of calligraphy. He employed a wriggling line, which changed from thick to thin, emphasizing movement and the contour of muscle. This technique was used to give the work life from a distance, necessary to the poster's primary function as advertisement. In Kiyonobu's masterful portrayals of the Kabuki actors, the actor and his role became one entity, with gestures captured in a precise form — a painted interpretation of the actor's role. Although he founded a clan which held virtual monopoly over the posters, programs and other announcements of the four theaters of Edo for several generations, few of the succeeding painters of the Torii clan would equal the powerful simplicity of the works of Kiyonobu I.

Theater Poster — Kichijuro Tsutsui Dancing the Spear-Dance, Nakamura Theater, Spring, 1704

In this vivid portrait, a Kabuki actor is in mid-performance of a dance invented by the actor Tatsunosuke Mizuki, who came to Edo in 1691 and was among the first actors to take a female role. This dance came to be adopted as an audition piece for all actors wishing to join the troupe of one of the established Edo theaters. The dance represents the ecstasy of the woman of the house in the rituals of cleaning and was well described in a poem by the poet Kikakudo, which translates: "Do you dream of flowers, Tatsunosuke, fluttering butterfly? Everybody dances with spears — no, with duster and polishing cloth — the joy of housecleaning."*

*Boller, W. *Masterpieces of the Japanese Woodcut.* Boston: Boston Book and Art Shop, 1957, p. 16.

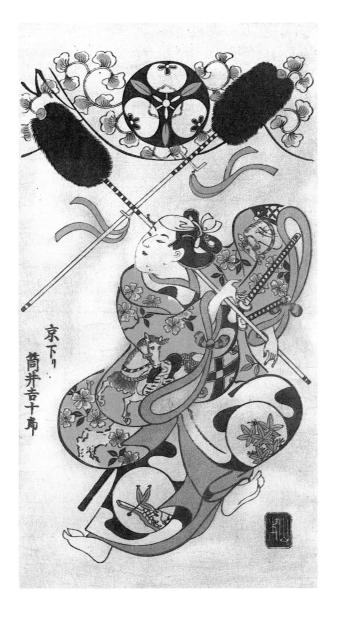

京下り
筒井吉十郎

TOYONOBU

During the time between the dominance of the Torii clan founded by Kiyonobu and the emergence of the artist Ishikawa Shuha Toyonobu (1711-1785), several important developments occurred in the art of the woodcut print. The artist Masonobu introduced the trademark stamp which would adorn the prints in the future, and also worked out several standard sizes, including the long, narrow *hashira-e* shape. In the history of ukiyo-e, the work of Toyonobu is considered to be late primitive in style. By this time, printing techniques had expanded to include *benizuri-e* — red-printed pictures — in which several colors could be printed from different blocks without laborious hand-painting. Toyonobu married the daughter of an inn-keeper and later became the proprietor of the inn himself. It was the carefree, robust atmosphere of the inn, where Toyonobu enjoyed the reputation of being one of the handsomest men in Edo, that provided him with much of his subject matter. There, surrounded by family and friends, the artist worked, creating his own vigorous style and portraying the women, young men, actors and other travelers who frequented his inn. He produced many books, and also innumerable single prints, preferring the long hashira shape invented by Masanobu and becoming a master of the *kakemono-e,* hanging scrolls weighted at the bottom, which were used to adorn pillars and the panels of screens. Toyonobu was a master of the nude figure, a subject little used by Japanese artists, but loved to depict changing styles of dress, and through his work one can follow the increasing popularity of the flowered patterns from the Kyoto textile houses, which superceded the geometric patterns of Edo fabrics. Throughout his long career, Toyonobu experimented with the new techniques of the day, moving from the simple handcolored print, through the *urishi-e,* the lacquer pictures mixed with glue, to the *benizuri-e,* or red-pictures, of which he was an acknowledged master, and finally, at the end of his life, producing full-color pictures using the new technique of *ushiki-e,* or multi-color printings. Toyonobu died at the age of 74 and was buried in the Shokaku Temple.

Woman with Scroll

This kakemono-e, or hanging scroll, of a courtesan reading a letter, is typical of Toyonobu's delicate sense of line and illustrates the subtleties that had been introduced into the ukiyo-e since the work of Moronobu. This is a hand-colored print, with delicate gray, blue and red tones in the kimono and the white scroll silhouetted against the pale tan of the background. The pattern of the kimono indicates that this fabric was one of the new textiles imported from Kyoto. The sensuous line and large color masses that influenced the French Impressionists a century later are clearly evident here.

HARUNOBU

The emergence of the technique of *nishiki-e,* or brocade pictures, which did so much to change the nature and appearance of Japanese woodcuts, is largely credited to Harunobu, born Hozumi Jibee (1725-1770), an artist who not only took advantage of all available new techniques, adding some of his own, but produced subject matter of unsurpassed delicacy. His portraits of women broke new ground in that they did not confine themselves to the oiran (coutesans) of the Yoshiwara district, although these figured often in his work, but also portrayed women closer to home, who worked in tea shops or lived around the corner. He chose as his models the most beautiful young girls, romanticizing them and endowing them with poetic, almost mystical grace. Many of his scenes were taken from ancient Chinese and Japanese tracts which he often illustrated in allegorical fashion. He incorporated lines of poetry into his works, placing his figures to accommodate the written words. He was also the first to incorporate human figures into realistic backgrounds, choosing soft tints of gray and green for these backgrounds, rather than the usual white. In 1765, in honor of the 900th anniversary of the master calligrapher and statesman Sugawara Michizane, graphic clubs and societies were founded which popularized the woodcut while they financed expensive private editions. The years 1765 and 1766 saw the first nishiki-e publications, in the form of private editions for collectors and connoisseurs. The first widespread publications of single full-color prints occurred in 1766 and were greatly acclaimed. Having founded his own publishing firm, Suzuki House, in 1760, Harunobu was both artist and businessman, and well able to take advantage of the new techniques for multi-color printing, the combined matte and glazed finishes, embossing, the better papers and improved inks, and the more highly-skilled craftsmen which were all now available. These culminated in his *Azuma-nishiki-e* — the Eastern Province (Edo) Brocade Pictures. During the last five years of his life, Harunobu took advantage of the success of the nishiki-e to produce many books and over 700 single-sheet prints in his romantic, idealized style, making him, before his untimely death from illness in 1770, one of the most successful masters of the ukiyo-e.

The Oiran Hinatsuru

This lovely composition shows us the oiran (courtesan) Hinatsuru — whose name means Young Crane, an apt description of her slender willowy figure — from the Choki-ya (Clove House). The young courtesan is seen here with two of her *kamuro* (servant-apprentices), enjoying the delights of the winter season. The younger girl is painting the eye of a snow sculpture while she holds a stone in her hands, probably for the pupil of the eye. The work is typically Harunobu's, remarkable for its realistic background, the innocent expressions of his young women, and the tender and romantic subject matter. The almost square shape of the work was preferred by him for most of his compositions.

KORYUSAI

The life of the almost legendary samurai painter Isoda Shobei, who painted under the name of Koryusai, is still clouded in mystery. Certain facts are known about his life: that his signature includes the prefix Hokkyo, a title given to honored priests; that he worked as a woodcut master from 1765-1780, and that he gave this up in favor of painting from 1780-1788. It is also known that he began his life as a samurai in the service of Lord Tsuchiya, but came to Edo as a *ronin,* a discharged mercenary, in a time when the ruling shogun had established a peaceful country in which the great battles between samurai warriors were only a distant memory. In Edo, the young samurai befriended the gentle, poetic artist, Harunobu, and worked so closely with him that for several generations scholars confused their work. Viewed today, their styles are clearly different. Koryusai's work is distinctive for its forcefulness and energy, quite unlike Harunobu's gentle and peaceful subjects. Koryusai achieved remarkable animal portraits, masterful in their barely controlled ferocity or sense of mischief. Other favorite subjects included historical figures, the oiran of the Yoshiwara brothels or "green houses," and shungas, erotic works. He often adopted the very long and narrow hashira format and used this shape to paint his "dream pictures," in which a woman sits in the bottom half of the picture, her dream in a cloud-like scene above her head. He is known for his single-print illustrations; no books have been attributed to his name. Koryusai developed a female prototype—women whose countenances and physical bearing resemble the more primitive works of Moronobu, but who wear a distinctive hair-style with protruding wings designed by Koryusai. A generation later, Kiyonaga used this hair-style for his own female figures, which came to be considered the ultimate feminine ideal. Although the work that has been attributed to him places Koryusai among the foremost masters of the ukiyo-e woodcut, no further details have been unearthed about his life; after paintings that can be dated from 1788, we know nothing about what became of the samurai artist.

Autumn
In this work, Koryusai's distinctively strong colors—deep blue, weighted by heavy black areas and punctuated by patches of beni-red, an orange color—are evident, as is his characteristic hair-style—the two wings extending out to the sides. The figure is placed in a barely indicated background, an attempt, perhaps, to individualize his work from that of Harunobu and other contemporary artists who were increasingly concerned with naturalistic settings. In this picture the season is portrayed through the most subtle of visual gestures—a few lines indicating the gusting wind which sweeps into the extended umbrella and through the branches of the tree. The graceful curve of the woman's body is echoed by the branches of the tree and balanced by the umbrella in a composition of pleasing harmony.

SHUNSHO

Katsukawa Shunsho (1726-1792), founder of the Katsukawa school, began his career in very humble circumstances, producing actors' portraits for his master in return for room and board. In 1768, however, a series of actors' portraits produced for the Kabuki troupe at the Nakamura Theater brought him overnight success, and Shunsho rose to prominence among ukiyo-e woodcut designers. Two years later, in collaboration with the artist, Buncho, he followed this success with the publication of the Fan Book—a series of half-length portraits on white fans against a blue background which featured Edo's most celebrated actors. This book has historical significance both for its documentation of Kabuki theater at the time, and as a milestone in the emerging art of theatrical portraiture. The publication of this book made quite a social splash as well, as the artists were honored by their publishers with the Thousand Prints Feast. In his portraits, Shunsho has clearly broken with the tradition of actor portraits carried on by the Torii clan founded by Kiyonobu. Shunsho's portraits are not stereotypes of an actor's role; they are clearly and unmistakably portraits of specific actors presented with an eye toward realism. Also evident in Shunsho's work is a growing concern with color, not as traditional representation, but presented for its various pleasing or striking effects. Shunsho's actor portraits, however, have little feeling of human concern for the men themselves. In fact, Shunsho, who purported to be descended from aristocratic lineage, rather scorned actors when they were not appearing on the stage and disclaimed any association with them. Shunsho's work was not limited to actor portraits; he also illustrated many books, shungas and pictures of the Yoshiwara women, including, in collaboration with Shigemasa, the handsome book "Mirror of Beautiful Women of the Green Houses," in which he sought an ideal of feminine perfection. In the opinion of most scholars, this ideal was finally achieved in the work of Kiyonaga. When Kiyonaga was named the fourth master of the prestigious Torii clan, Shunsho, apparently disappointed, abandoned the woodcut medium and returned to classical painting, which he practiced until his death in 1792.

The Actor Danjuro V in the part of the Shinozuka Iga

Danjuro V, a leading actor of the Nakamura Theater, was among the best of his day, and was featured in many of Shunsho's works. This portrait, one of at least eight painted of the same actor in this part, is one of Shunsho's strongest, and captures Danjuro's virile force and sense of restrained ferocity. The realistic portrayal of the actor, who could not be taken for anyone but himself, and the striking use of color—the bold red offset by geometric patterns of white—attest to Shunsho's mastery of technique and his innovative concept of portraiture.

UTAMARO

Utamaro (1754-1806) was, like his contemporary, Kiyonaga, a master of the golden age of ukiyo-e, and like Kiyonaga, concentrated his attention on the beautiful courtesans of the Yoshiwara "green houses." He, too, developed a "distinctive" woman, a female of charm and grace. But despite the popularity of his work, his considerable reputation and his prolific output, Utamaro's life was fraught with difficulty. He was apprenticed at twenty-three to Toriyama Sekien and by the time of the death of his master, Utamaro had already established his reputation with the publication of an illustrated book of poetry on the subject of insects. He was soon taken in hand by Tsutaya Jusaburo, a publisher with an eye for young talent. Tsutaya kept the young artist securely employed and relatively well-paid during his entire career, but this relationship was often a mixed blessing. Although his work was successful, Utamaro's extravagances often had him in financial difficulty and dependent upon his publisher, binding the artist even more tightly to what he at times felt was a restricting commitment. Utamaro attempted throughout his career to capture the fleeting and haunting beauty of nature, whether in an animal, a tree, or a beautiful woman. He lived at the entrance of the Yoshiwara district and when he was thirty-three, married a young girl of great beauty who often modeled for him and helped with his work. However, at the height of his career, he came into disfavor with a government censor who objected to one of his satirical works, and Utamaro was sent to prison, where his health was seriously undermined. He died soon after his release. Utamaro's output was prodigious, perhaps in a frantic attempt to keep pace with his personal extravagances. By the time of his death he had produced over 600 books and albums of prints. His most famous work consists of studies of the Yoshiwara women, who were culled from the most beautiful young girls in Japan and trained as carefully as the most skilled court princesses. Although the oiran of the Yoshiwara formed the subject matter of all the ukiyo-e artists, nowhere are they more celebrated than in the work of Utamaro.

Powdering the Neck

This portrait of one of the oiran of the Yoshiwara "green houses," is remarkable for its simplicity of form, boldness of composition and for the exquisite loveliness of the courtesan. The nape of the neck was a portion of the female anatomy held in high esteem by Japanese lovers of feminine beauty, and the three-quarter view was the one considered the most flattering and desirable. This view of a courtesan powdering her neck is a three-quarter view in reverse. The poem in the upper left hand corner compares the graceful line of her neck, her hairpin and her white powdered face to a snowy, moonlit landscape. Perhaps more than any other artist of the Yoshiwara courtesans, Utamaro was known for the love and devotion he felt for these beautiful and accomplished women, whom he celebrated in his art. In this particular composition, however, it is also important to note the clean line, bold forms and large color masses which were to have such a striking influence on the Western artists of the next century.

SHARAKU

Another contemporary of Kiyonaga and Utamaro during the golden age of the ukiyo-e was Toshusai Sharaku, an artist who literally burst on the scene for a whirlwind ten months during the season from 1794 to 1795, and then disappeared from the artistic world completely. Among the mysteries that surround the lives of many of the ukiyo-e artists, Sharaku's is the most famous and the most puzzling. In May of 1794, a Noh actor from the city of Awa named Saito Jurobei approached Edo's largest publisher, Tsutaya Jusaburo, and offered his services. Two months later, Tsutaya House published a series of luxury prints — thirty-one portraits of Kabuki actors in large scale, an amazing output in such a short time — in a deluxe edition decorated with mica and silver backgrounds and signed by an unknown artist, Toshusai Sharaku. These portraits are marked by an extreme realism in facial expression, which was taken for caricature at the time. This first portfolio created quite a stir and its very notoriety drew the attention of government censors, who banned the lavishness of these theater posters. Although the first edition proved a financial disaster for the publisher after the government bans, he nevertheless believed in the artist enough to offer him more commissions. The second set of posters, small in scale, concentrated on movement and gestures of the actors, but these and the prints that followed were poorly received; eventually, after 300 days and 145 woodcuts, publisher and artist abandoned the project. Sharaku, evidently discouraged by his poor reception, retired as an artist and most likely returned to Awa, for a list of Noh players from the year 1825 contains the name Saito Jurobei. Nothing else was ever heard of him again; the name Sharaku disappeared completely from Edo and dates of his birth and death are unknown. It is especially interesting that his woodcuts, which were so unpopular in Japan, were the first to attract the attention of European and American collectors: the intense psychological impact of the facial expressions, which had disconcerted the Japanese, was the very element which was most appealing in the West. The power of these portraits creates a visual impact totally apart from the placement of form or color, an artistic concept alien at the time to the Eastern mind but which had great meaning in Europe and America.

Portrait of the Actor Bando Mitsugoro II as Ishii Genzo

This portrait depicts the actor in a Kabuki play given at the Miyako-za theater in May of 1794, and is one of the portraits in the first portfolio of thirty-one, 23 single sheet and 7 double sheet, that introduced the work of Sharaku to an outraged public. The most striking element of these portraits, the intense facial expressions combined with a realistic attention to the characteristics of individual actors, both marked them as an innovative new departure, and horrified the majority of the print-buying public. That this was a deluxe edition, produced with much care, can be seen in the subtle coloration, the mica background, and the embossed texture of the actor's white garment. It was this same lavishness that brought down the wrath of the censors on this ill-starred project.

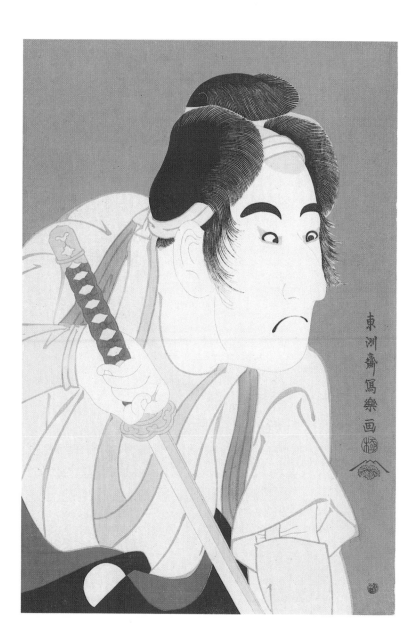

TOYOHARU

Utagawa Toyoharu (1733-1814), the founder of the Utagawa school of artists whose later members included Hiroshige and Kuniyoshi, was born in Toyooka on the island of Kyushu and studied painting in Kyoto before moving to Edo. Toyoharu's style of drawing was lively and original, intricately composed and known for narrative detail. Although his early work is reminiscent of Toyonobu, in the 1770s Toyoharu began to design uki-e (perspective prints), incorporating Western ideas of perspective and shading. These were innovative pictures of Venice and other foreign cities based on Dutch copperplate engravings. During this period, which may be described as a time of decline in the arts, the shogunate was exercising a repressive censorship, and many traditional subjects, such as the Kabuki and Yoshiwara, were banned. This repression led to an increased restlessness in the arts and with it came an interest in the foreign influences slowly infiltrating Japan. The great popularity of Toyoharu's uki-e is indicative of the widening horizon of Japan at this time, the slowly lifting cloud of isolation. The intellectual classes rapidly embraced all knowledge that filtered into the country through the Dutch on their early voyages, although a true exchange of ideas would not occur for almost another century. In addition to the uki-e, Toyoharu was also instrumental in the production of the popular nishiki-e, or brocade prints, with their rich coloration, a technique pioneered by Harunobu, but brought to its height by the artists of the Utagawa school. Although Toyoharu did not remain a well-known name among Ukiyo-e artists, his pupils Toyokuni, Kuniyoshi and especially Hiroshige, would uphold the honor of the Utagawa techniques. In addition to his work as a printmaker, Toyoharu was a fine painter of ukiyo-e subjects. His career was short, however, for in 1785 he gave up painting and print-making and became a monk, living in a monastery until his death in 1814.

Interior and Winter Landscape: a Gay Party, Men and Geishas

This work is interesting for its sense of an exterior landscape in an interior scene, imparted by the large panel behind the figures in the center of the room. The work is intricately composed: many figures share a small space, yet diagonal lines of the floor and at the base of the panel add the illusion of depth. Many intimate details of life in the Yoshiwara houses are in evidence here: the utensils used in the tea ceremony, the *samisen* or Japanese lute, trays, mats, house slippers. These familiar objects, along with the relaxed poses of the figures, evoke a feeling of being privileged to an intimate glimpse of everyday life. The rich coloration in this scene of a Yoshiwara "green house" is typical of the nishiki-e or brocade print, a sophisticated technique that well illustrates the progress made since the original hand-colored woodcuts of Moronubu and Kiyonobu.

TOYOHIRO

Utagawa Toyohiro (1763-1828), was one of the most gifted students of Toyoharu, founder of the Utagawa school of woodcut artists. During his lifetime, government censorship by the now desperate shogunate, which sensed the end of its period of hegemony, had drained the ukiyo-e masters of much of their vitality. The masters Toyohiro and Toyokuni, who might have made a major contribution, were restricted on all sides from any significant changes in style or technique and were confined to refining their master's art. If any criticism can be made of Toyohiro's work, it is this lack of innovation; yet his work is still notable for its lyric grace and gentleness, and for the many genre details it recorded of everyday life. Since Toyohiro was a teacher of both painting and wood engraving, it is possible that he executed many of the steps in the complex process of woodcut engraving himself. He is noted for his series of prints: many of Yoshiwara women engaged in daily activities; some of historical events; some of landscape scenes, and others, particularly interesting, of the local products that were proudly displayed at the stations and markets along the Tokaido river trade route from Edo to Kyoto. It was this same trade route that Hiroshige would later make famous in his landscape studies. Throughout these varying subjects, Toyohiro's work retains its quiet, graceful quality. Series of his works bear such titles as "The Four Accomplishments," "The Four Amusements," "The Three Cities," "The Six Great Poets," and "The Twelve Hours." It was as a teacher, however, that Toyohiro is perhaps the most well known, and among his students was a prodigy who would become the best landscape artist of his time, and indeed, one of the most exalted masters of ukiyo-e: Hiroshige.

The Four Accomplishments, No. 2
This is one of a pair of panels depicting the basic skills necessary to an accomplished oiran, or courtesan. The first panel illustrates two types of calligraphy—brush painting and the writing of poetry. This second panel illustrates the playing of a musical instrument and skill at indoor games. In the foregound, an oiran is assisted by her kamuro, or apprentice. The oiran in the background is entertaining a visitor at a game. When placed together the positioning of the figures in the left and right panel of this diptych, or two-panel painting, forms a circular composition. In the receding perspective indicated by the open door and the landscape in the background, we can see a touch of the Western influence typical of the Utagawa school of this period.

HOKUSAI

Katsushika Hokusai (1760-1849), the best known and most loved of all the ukiyo-e masters, was born in a suburb of Edo, the son of a mirror-grinder, and throughout his long life, it was in the houses of artisans and common workmen that he felt the most comfortable. Apprenticed to Shunsho, the master of theatrical portraits, Hokusai had trouble accepting the rigidity of his teachers and studied ancient Chinese and Japanese painting, eventually renouncing the name of his master. Throughout his life, Hokusai was uninterested in money and fame and ignored the comfort and security his reputation could easily have secured him, choosing instead a path of constant striving after perfection. He was never satisfied with what he considered his facility, but sought to bring a truer meaning to his art. He was a prodigious worker and experimented with new ideas and subject matter, writing novels and poetry and illustrating his books. He produced an ambitious set of notebooks, known as the *Manga* — some fifteen volumes of sketches which covered all forms of subject matter: landscapes, animal and nature studies, ghost pictures, studies of the human form in all poses and many grotesque distortions, and even schematic studies of Western theories of perspective. In the *Manga* Hokusai hoped to provide a source book for artists as well as a record of his own studies. This *Manga,* when it finally made its way to Europe, had an extraordinary influence on European artists. During his life, Hokusai lived at some ninety different locations and adopted five different aliases, repeatedly overcoming the most wretched poverty and distress. One of the great achievements of his career, a series of thirty-six studies of Mount Fuji, was accomplished when Hokusai was in his 60s. His assessment of his work at this time states that all his achievements before the age of 70 are inconsequential; that at 80 and 90 years of age he would be making slow progress toward an understanding of what it means to be an artist, possibly reaching his goal by the age of 100. Hokusai never stopped experimenting with new techniques and many believe that it was between the ages of 80 and 90 that the old man produced his finest work, including his "color book" in which he advised students to follow their own truth rather than submit to the dictates of fashion. He died at the age of 90 in a house not far from the one where he was born, still feeling that he had not yet reached the threshhold of greatness as an artist.

The Ono Waterfall on the Kiso Road (1827)

This subject is one of a series entitled "The Waterfalls," done during the period of the Fuji series. In Hokusai's work, landscape was no longer a backdrop to human activities, rather it was the human figures which became part of the harmonious grandeur of landscape. Hokusai incorporated in his woodcuts both the techniques of Japanese and Chinese brush painting, seen here in the clouds which seem to float in and out of the foreground, and modified techniques of Western perspective, as evidenced by the slightly receding lines of the waterfalls and the hills behind the descending roadway. Hokusai did not take his landscapes directly from nature, building instead harmonious structures from his own inner vision.

28

HIROSHIGE

Ichiryusai Hiroshige (1797-1858), forty years younger than Hokusai, is often considered the last great ukiyo-e artist, and is certainly the one who brought the art of landscape painting to its greatest heights, studying and working directly from nature in travels around Japan. His works are remarkable for their subtlety of coloration, achieving atmospheric effects with a minimum of gesture and color. By the end of Hiroshige's life, the ships of Commodore Perry had arrived, opening the door to a rash of Western influences and bringing the end of an era. The reign of the shogunal government was over and so was the time of the nishiki-e, which could no longer compete in the popular marketplace with new techniques of photography and lithography. Hiroshige's works are among the first to be directly imported to Europe and would influence European artists greatly, as well as instructing the Western mind about matters Japanese. Hiroshige was born Tokitaro Ando, near the seashore in Edo, the son of a member of the fire police. He showed talent at a young age and was placed in the studio of Toyohiro; by the time he was fifteen, he had received his Utagawa master's certificate and the name Utagawa Hiroshige, the first syllable of Hiroshige taken from the last syllable of his master's name, in the Utagawa tradition. With the death of Toyohiro in 1829, Hiroshige left the studio to take up his true vocation of landscape painting. He married the daughter of a samurai and took up the post of river inspector, one of the guild jobs of the fire police, a job which well suited him as it allowed him to travel to all the Tokaido provinces and study the landscape under varying conditions. Hiroshige's first major accomplishments as a landscape painter were of subjects along the Tokaido river trade route which connected the cities of Edo and Kyoto. These river scenes, published as the Tokaido series, established his reputation. Hiroshige pioneered a new concept in art in which color replaced line as the primary element. In this and in his notion of landscapes painted directly from nature, Hiroshige sounds a note familiar to Western painters, for these are the foundations of the Impressionist philosophy which would shake French art in the next generation; yet Hiroshige's art also echoes all the themes of the Japanese classical tradition with its love of peaceful harmony and contemplation. Hiroshige died of cholera in 1858 and his loss was felt by many.

Wild Duck

This striking picture of a wild duck is typical of Hiroshige's remarkable economy of expression. Subtle gradations of color rather than line are the predominant element in the print and tell the story of a raw winter day hushed by the falling snow. The poem in the upper left-hand corner of the picture adds to the experience:

"The wind blows over the water
And cold grips us and solitude
When the wild duck cries.*

*Boller, W. Masterpieces of the Japanese Color Woodcut. Boston: Boston Book and Art Shop, 1957. p. 178.